MOURNING SONGS

MOURNING SONGS

Poems of Sorrow and Beauty

Edited by Grace Schulman

Acknowledgments and permissions for the poems in this volume can be
found beginning on page 140.

Manufactured in the United States of America
New Directions Books are printed on acid-free paper.
First published as a New Directions Paperbook Original (NDP1447) in 2019
Design by Marian Bantjes

Library of Congress Cataloging-in-Publication Data
Names: Schulman, Grace, editor.
Title: Mourning songs : poems of sorrow and beauty / edited by Grace
Schulman.
Description: New York, New York : New Directions Publishing
Corporation, 2019. | "A New Directions paperbook original."
Identifiers: LCCN 2019001470 | ISBN 9780811228664 (alk. paper)
Subjects: LCSH: Death—Poetry. | Bereavement—Poetry. | Grief—Poetry.
Classification: LCC PN6110.D4 M58 2019 | DDC 808.81/93548—dc23
LC record available at https://lccn.loc.gov/2019001470

10 9 8 7 6 5 4 3 2 1

New Directions Books are published for James Laughlin
by New Directions Publishing Corporation
80 Eighth Avenue, NY 10011

TABLE OF CONTENTS

10 Introduction

For the Beloved

13 *The Widow's Lament in Springtime*
William Carlos Williams (1883–1963)

15 *The River-Merchant's Wife: A Letter*
Ezra Pound (1885–1972)

17 *Rain Light* W. S. Merwin (1927–2019)

18 *Do Not Go Gentle into That Good Night*
Dylan Thomas (1914–1953)

20 *On My First Son* Ben Jonson (1572–1637)

21 *The Rites for Cousin Vit*
Gwendolyn Brooks (1917–2000)

22 *Never More Will the Wind*
H. D. (Hilda Doolittle) (1886–1961)

23 *Mourning Chao* Li Po (701–762)

24 *The Cross of Snow*
Henry Wadsworth Longfellow (1807–1882)

25 *Alberto Rojas Jiménez Comes Flying*
Pablo Neruda (1904–1973)

Time to Plant Tears

31 *Sestina* Elizabeth Bishop (1911–1979)

33 *Remember Me When I Am Gone Away*
Christina Rossetti (1830–1894)

34 *Remembrance* Emily Brontë (1818–1848)

36 *Elegy for Jane* Theodore Roethke (1908–1963)

38 *Ave Atque Vale* James Laughlin (1914–1997)

40 *The Last Words of My English Grandmother*
William Carlos Williams

42 *Requiem* Ryszard Krynicki (1943–)

43 *For My Brother: Reported Missing in Action,
1943* Thomas Merton (1915–1968)

45 *Catullus 101* (84–54 BCE)

46 from *In Memoriam A.H.H.*
Alfred Lord Tennyson (1809–1892)

48 *A Refusal to Mourn the Death, by Fire,
of a Child in London* Dylan Thomas

50 *Redemption Song* Kevin Young (1970–)

53 *Last Requests* Grace Schulman (1935–)

Hymns, Psalms, and Laments

56 *Dirge* (from *Cymbeline*)
William Shakespeare (1582–1616)

58 *Lyke-Wake Dirge* Trad. English

60 *Shall We Gather at the River*
Robert Lowry (1826–1854)

62 *Women's Dance Song*   Native American

63 *Psalms*   King James Version

66 *Kaddish*

The Shape of Death

68 *Evening*   H. D. (Hilda Doolittle)

69 *What Are Years*   Marianne Moore (1887–1972)

71 *Death Be Not Proud*   John Donne (1572–1631)

72 *After Great Pain*   Emily Dickinson
(1839–1886)

73 *And Death Shall Have No Dominion*
Dylan Thomas

75 *Books, Paintings*   Ryszard Krynicki

76 *In the Home of the Dead Man*
Llujeta Lleshanaku (1968–)

77 *Question*   May Swenson (1913–1989)

Talking to Grief

79 *Chamomile Breath*   Llujeta Lleshanaku

81 *Talking to Grief*   Denise Levertov (1923–1997)

82 *Rider's Song*   Federico García Lorca
(1898–1936)

83 *No Worst, There is None*
Gerard Manley Hopkins (1844–1889)

84 *When I Have Fears That I May Cease to Be*
John Keats (1795–1821)

85 *Not to Die Now*   Allen Grossman (1932–2014)

86 *Only Death*   Pablo Neruda

89 *Nothing Gold Can Stay*   Robert Frost
(1874–1963)

90 *I Live Yet Do Not Live in Me*
St. John of the Cross (1452–1591)

93 *A Lamentation*   Denise Levertov

95 *How Do I Love Thee*
Elizabeth Barrett Browning (1806–1846)

96 *The Heavy Bear Who Goes With Me*
Delmore Schwartz (1913–1966)

End of Days

99 *This Living Hand, Now Warm and Capable*
John Keats

100 *Even Such is Time*   Sir Walter Raleigh
(1552–1618)

101 *Requiem*   Robert Louis Stevenson (1880–1894)

102 *Epitaph*   Samuel Taylor Coleridge (1772–1834)

103 *Last Request*   Michael Palmer (1943–)

105 from *Doctor Faustus*   Christopher Marlowe
(1564–1593)

For the Masters

109 *September 1961*   Denise Levertov

112 *Joseph Brodsky's Grave*   Ryszard Krynicki

114 *Elegy for Thelonious*   Yusef Komunyakaa (1947–)

116 *At Melville's Tomb*   Hart Crane (1899–1932)

117 *In Memory of W. B. Yeats*   W. H. Auden (1903–1973)

121 from *When Lilacs Last in the Dooryard Bloom'd*   Walt Whitman (1819–1892)

For the World

126 *Requiem*   Bei Dao (1948–)

128 *What Were They Like*   Denise Levertov

130 *Anthem for Doomed Youth*   Wilfred Owen (1893–1918)

131 *A Litany in Time of Plague*   Thomas Nashe (1567–1601)

133 *Campo dei Fiori*   Csezlaw Milosz (1911–2004)

136 *Reconciliation*   Walt Whitman

137 *To a Dog Injured in the Street*   William Carlos Williams

140 *The Darkling Thrush*   Thomas Hardy (1840–1928)

W. H. Auden asserted that all poetry must "praise all it can for being and happening," an observation that is borne out in the poetry of grief and death. Religion, too, calls upon praise for the theme of death rituals. In Judaism, the Kaddish, said at funerals, is a hymn of praise in the language of Aramaic without a word of death. In the Muslim tradition, the Imam asks for Allah praise, thanksgiving, and glorification.

Praise recurs throughout the Book of Psalms, which clerics tell mourners to read for comfort, and Psalm 42, often recited at Anglican burial services, sings of praise and thanksgiving. The death rituals of many cultures is called a "wake," often accompanied by merry talk, dance and song. And, liveliest of all, brass bands in New Orleans play hot jazz after the church services, a custom known as "the second line beat." On the streets people dance with open umbrellas.

Poetry has its origin in prayer, and neither poetry nor prayer can bandage grief's wounds. As any bereaved survivor knows, there is no consolation. "Time doesn't heal grief; it emphasizes it," wrote Marianne Moore. The loss of a loved one never leaves us. We don't want it to. In grief, one remembers the beloved. But running beside it, parallel to it, is the joy of existence, the love that causes pain of loss, the loss that enlarges us with the wonder of existence.

The poems in this collection sing of grief as they praise life. But praise goes down many avenues, as does loss. Here, personal sorrows range from the ancient Catullus to the moderns Dylan Thomas and Gwendolyn Brooks. The great poets are mourned by the Elizabethan Ben Jonson, the modern Denise Levertov, and the contemporaries Mary Karr and Yusef Komunyakaa. Public terror, the grief for those unknown, is passionately expressed by the ageless Whitman, the war poet Wilfred Owen and the brave ones of our time, such as Luljeta Lleshanaku and Ryszard Krynicki. There are discoveries to be made in combining them: ironically, or marvelously, those poets with a sensibility to suffering are clearly attuned to personal imagery, speech, and rhythm. They zealously hold to their individuality despite public grief. At times those in sorrow call upon living, growing things to assuage their grief, as though the things of this world can raise up our determination to live.

All the poems here are celebrations of life. The very act of writing a poem, of putting pen to paper or, nowadays, printing it from a computer, is an act of praising the will to live. Poetry affirms that will.

Grace Schulman
New York, NY

For the Beloved

THE WIDOW'S LAMENT IN SPRINGTIME

Sorrow is my own yard
where the new grass
flames as it has flamed
often before, but not
with the cold fire
that closes round me this year.
Thirty-five years
I lived with my husband.
The plum tree is white today
with masses of flowers.
Masses of flowers
load the cherry branches
and color some bushes
yellow and some red,
but the grief in my heart
is stronger than they,
for though they were my joy
formerly, today I notice them
and turn away forgetting.
Today my son told me
that in the meadows,
at the edge of the heavy woods
in the distance, he saw
trees of white flowers.
I feel that I would like

to go there
and fall into those flowers
and sink into the marsh near them.

William Carlos Williams

THE RIVER-MERCHANT'S WIFE: A LETTER
After Li Po

While my hair was still cut straight across my
    forehead
I played about the front gate, pulling flowers.
You came by on bamboo stilts, playing horse,
You walked about my seat, playing with blue
    plums.
And we went on living in the village of Chōkan:
Two small people, without dislike or suspicion.
At fourteen I married My Lord you.
I never laughed, being bashful.
Lowering my head, I looked at the wall.
Called to, a thousand times, I never looked back.

At fifteen I stopped scowling,
I desired my dust to be mingled with yours
Forever and forever, and forever.
Why should I climb the look out?

At sixteen you departed
You went into far Ku-tō-en, by the river of
    swirling eddies,
And you have been gone five months.
The monkeys make sorrowful noise overhead.

You dragged your feet when you went out.
By the gate now, the moss is grown, the different
    mosses,

Too deep to clear them away!
The leaves fall early this autumn, in wind.
The paired butterflies are already yellow with
        August
Over the grass in the West garden;
They hurt me.
I grow older.
If you are coming down through the narrows of
        the river Kiang,
Please let me know beforehand,
And I will come out to meet you
As far as Chō-fū-Sa.

Ezra Pound

RAIN LIGHT

All day the stars watch from long ago
my mother said I am going now
when you are alone you will be all right
whether or not you know you will know
look at the old house in the dawn rain
all the flowers are forms of water
the sun reminds them through a white cloud
touches the patchwork spread on the hill
the washed colors of the afterlife
that lived there long before you were born
see how they wake without a question
even though the whole world is burning

W. S. Merwin

DO NOT GO GENTLE INTO THAT GOOD NIGHT

Do not go gentle into that good night,
Old age should burn and rave at close of day;
Rage, rage against the dying of the light.

Though wise men at their end know dark is right,
Because their words had forked no lightning they
Do not go gentle into that good night.

Good men, the last wave by, crying how bright
Their frail deeds might have danced in a green
        bay,
Rage, rage against the dying of the light.

Wild men who caught and sang the sun in flight,
And learn, too late, they grieved it on its way,
Do not go gentle into that good night.

Grave men, near death, who see with blinding
        sight
Blind eyes could blaze like meteors and be gay,
Rage, rage against the dying of the light.

And you, my father, there on the sad height,
Curse, bless, me now with your fierce tears, I
        pray.

Do not go gentle into that good night.
Rage, rage against the dying of the light

Dylan Thomas

ON MY FIRST SON

Farewell, thou child of my right hand, and joy;
My sin was too much hope of thee, lov'd boy.
Seven years thou wert lent to me, and I thee pay,
Exacted by thy fate, on the just day.
O, could I lose all father now! For why
Will man lament the state he should envy?
To have so soon 'scap'd world's and flesh's rage,
And if no other misery, yet age?
Rest in soft peace, and, ask'd, say, "Here doth lie
Ben Jonson his best piece of poetry."
For whose sake henceforth all his vows be such,
As what he loves may never like too much.

Ben Jonson

Carried her unprotesting out the door.
Kicked back the casket-stand. But it can't hold
      her,
That stuff and satin aiming to enfold her,
The lid's contrition nor the bolts before.
Oh oh. Too much. Too much. Even now, surmise,
She rises in the sunshine. There she goes,
Back to the bars she knew and the repose
In love-rooms and the things in people's eyes.
Too vital and too squeaking. Must emerge.
Even now she does the snake-hips with a hiss,
Slops the bad wine across her shantung, talks
Of pregnancy, guitars and bridgework, walks
In parks or alleys, comes haply on the verge
Of happiness, haply hysterics. Is.

Gwendolyn Brooks

NEVER MORE WILL THE WIND

Never more will the wind
cherish you again,
never more will the rain.

Never more
shall we find you bright
in the snow and wind.

The snow is melted,
the snow is gone,
and you are flown:

Like a bird out of our hand,
like a light out of our heart,
you are gone.

H. D. (Hilda Doolittle)

MOURNING CHAO

Chao left our imperial city for his Japanese
    homeland,
a lone flake of sail. Now he wanders islands of
    immortals.

Foundering in emerald seas, a bright moon never
    to return
leaves white, grief-tinged clouds crowding our
    southlands.

Li Po
Translated from the Chinese
by David Hinton

THE CROSS OF SNOW

In the long, sleepless watches of the night,
    A gentle face—the face of one long dead—
    Looks at me from the wall, where round its
       head
    The night-lamp casts a halo of pale light.
Here in this room she died; and soul more white
    Never through martyrdom of fire was led
    To its repose; nor can in books be read
    The legend of a life more benedight.
There is a mountain in the distant West
    That, sun-defying, in its deep ravines
    Displays a cross of snow upon its side.
Such is the cross I wear upon my breast
    These eighteen years, through all the
       changing scenes
    And seasons, changeless since the day she
       died.

Henry Wadsworth Longfellow

ALBERTO ROJAS JIMENEZ COMES FLYING

Among frightening feathers, among nights,
among magnolias, among telegrams,
among the South wind and the maritime West,
      you come flying.

Beneath the tombs, beneath the ashes,
beneath the frozen snails,
beneath the last terrestrial waters,
      you come flying.

Farther down, among submerged girls,
and blind plants, and broken fish,
farther down, among clouds again,
      you come flying

Beyond blood and bones,
beyond bread, beyond wine
beyond fire,
      you come flying.

Beyond vinegar and death
among putrefaction and violets,
with your celestial voice and your damp shoes,
      you come flying.

Over delegations and drugstores,
and wheels, and lawyers, and warships,

and red teeth recently pulled,
     you come flying.

Over sunken-roofed cities
where huge women take down their hair
with broad hands and lost combs,
     you come flying.

Next to vaults where the wine grows
with tepid turbid hands, in silence,
with slow, red-wooden hands,
     you come flying.

Among vanished aviators,
beside canals and shadows,
beside buried lilies,
     you come flying.

Among bitter-colored bottles,
among rings of anise and misfortune,
lifting your hands and weeping,
     you come flying.

Over dentists and congregations,
over moviehouses and tunnels and ears,
with a new suit and extinguished eyes,
     you come flying.

Over your wall-less cemetery,
where sailors go astray,
while the rain of your death falls,
        you come flying.

While the rain of your fingers falls,
while the rain of your bones falls,
while your marrow and your laughter fall,
        you come flying.

Over the stones on which you melt,
running, down winter, down time,
while your heart descends in drops,
        you come flying.

You are not there, surrounded by cement,
and black hearts of notaries,
and infuriated riders' bones:
        you come flying.

Oh sea poppy, oh my kinsman
oh guitar player dressed in bees,
it's not true so much shadow in your hair:
        you come flying.

It's not true so much shadow pursuing you,
it's not true so many dead swallows,

so much region dark with laments:
     you come flying.

The black wind of Valparaiso
opens its wings of coal and foam
to sweep the sky where you pass:
     you come flying.

There are ships, and a dead-sea cold,
and whistles, and months, and a smell
of rainy morning and dirty fish:
     you come flying.

There is rum, you and I, and my heart where I
     weep,
and nobody, and nothing, but a staircase
of broken steps, and an umbrella:
     you come flying.

There lies the sea. I go down at night and I hear
     you
come flying under the sea without anyone,
under the sea that dwells in me, darkened:
     you come flying.

I hear your wings and your slow flight,
and the water of the dead strikes me

like blind wet doves:
      you come flying.

You come flying, alone, solitary
alone among the dead, forever alone,
you come flying without a shadow and without
      a name,
without sugar, without a mouth, without
      rosebushes,
      you come flying.

Pablo Neruda
Translated from the Spanish
by Donald D. Walsh

Time to Plant Tears

SESTINA

September rain falls on the house.
In the failing light, the old grandmother
sits in the kitchen with the child
beside the Little Marvel Stove,
reading the jokes from the almanac,
laughing and talking to hide her tears.

She thinks that her equinoctial tears
and the rain that beats on the roof of the house
were both foretold by the almanac,
but only known to a grandmother.
The iron kettle sings on the stove.
She cuts some bread and says to the child,

It's time for tea now; but the child
is watching the teakettle's small hard tears
dance like mad on the hot black stove,
the way the rain must dance on the house.
Tidying up, the old grandmother
hangs up the clever almanac

on its string. Birdlike, the almanac
hovers half open above the child,
hovers above the old grandmother
and her teacup full of dark brown tears.
She shivers and says she thinks the house
feels chilly, and puts more wood in the stove.

It was to be, says the Marvel Stove.
I know what I know, says the almanac.
With crayons the child draws a rigid house
and a winding pathway. Then the child
puts in a man with buttons like tears
and shows it proudly to the grandmother.

But secretly, while the grandmother
busies herself about the stove,
the little moons fall down like tears
from between the pages of the almanac
into the flower bed the child
has carefully placed in the front of the house.

Time to plant tears, says the almanac.
The grandmother sings to the marvelous stove
and the child draws another inscrutable house.

Elizabeth Bishop

REMEMBER ME WHEN I AM GONE AWAY

Remember me when I am gone away,
    Gone far away into the silent land;
    When you can no more hold me by the hand,
Nor I half turn to go yet turning stay.
Remember me when no more day by day
    You tell me of our future that you plann'd:
    Only remember me; you understand
It will be late to counsel then or pray.
Yet if you should forget me for a while
    And afterwards remember, do not grieve:
    For if the darkness and corruption leave
    A vestige of the thoughts that once I had,
Better by far you should forget and smile
    Than that you should remember and be sad.

Christina Rossetti

REMEMBRANCE

Cold in the earth—and the deep snow piled above
    thee,
Far, far removed, cold in the dreary grave!
Have I forgot, my only Love, to love thee,
Severed at last by Time's all-severing wave?

Now, when alone, do my thoughts no longer
    hover
Over the mountains, on that northern shore,
Resting their wings where heath and fern-leaves
    cover
Thy noble heart forever, ever more?

Cold in the earth—and fifteen wild Decembers,
From those brown hills, have melted into spring:
Faithful, indeed, is the spirit that remembers
After such years of change and suffering!

Sweet Love of youth, forgive, if I forget thee,
While the world's tide is bearing me along;
Other desires and other hopes beset me,
Hopes which obscure, but cannot do thee wrong!

No later light has lightened up my heaven,
No second morn has ever shone for me;
All my life's bliss from thy dear life was given,
All my life's bliss is in the grave with thee.

But, when the days of golden dreams had
    perished,
And even Despair was powerless to destroy,
Then did I learn how existence could be
    cherished,
Strengthened, and fed without the aid of joy.

Then did I check the tears of useless passion—
Weaned my young soul from yearning after
    thine;
Sternly denied its burning wish to hasten
Down to that tomb already more than mine.

And, even yet, I dare not let it languish,
Dare not indulge in memory's rapturous pain;
Once drinking deep of that divinest anguish,
How could I seek the empty world again?

Emily Brontë

ELEGY FOR JANE

(My student, thrown by a horse)

I remember the neckcurls, limp and damp as
      tendrils;
And her quick look, a sidelong pickerel smile;
And how, once startled into talk, the light
      syllables leaped for her,
And she balanced in the delight of her thought,
A wren, happy, tail into the wind,
Her song trembling the twigs and small
      branches.
The shade sang with her;
The leaves, their whispers turned to kissing,
And the mould sang in the bleached valleys
      under the rose.
Oh, when she was sad, she cast herself down into
      such a pure depth,
Even a father could not find her:
Scraping her cheek against straw,
Stirring the clearest water.
My sparrow, you are not here,
Waiting like a fern, making a spiney shadow.
The sides of wet stones cannot console me,
Nor the moss, wound with the last light.
If only I could nudge you from this sleep,
My maimed darling, my skittery pigeon.

Over this damp grave I speak the words of my
      love:
I, with no rights in this matter,
Neither father nor lover.

Theodore Roethke

AVE ATQUE VALE

My father

I sat on the edge of the bed
and held his hand   it was dry

and cold   I squeezed the hand
but of course there was no re-

sponse   they had dressed him
in one of his Scottish tweed

suits with the deer's-horn
buttons on the side pockets

and put on the Princeton
(orange and black) tie   I

had come to say goodbye   I
was crying but suddenly my

sadness changed to resent-
ment even to anger almost

to hatred   why are you de-
serting me   how dare you

leave me   in my rage I
pulled up his shoulders

and shook him as hard as
I could   I raised him

further and banged his head
against the pillow   I want-

ed to make him open his eyes
how can you abandon me   you

the one who loved me most.

James Laughlin

THE LAST WORDS
OF MY ENGLISH GRANDMOTHER

There were some dirty plates
and a glass of milk
beside her on a small table
near the rank, disheveled bed—

Wrinkled and nearly blind
she lay and snored
rousing with anger in her tones
to cry for food,

Gimme something to eat—
They're starving me—
I'm all right-I won't go
to the hospital. No, no, no

Give me something to eat!
Let me take you
to the hospital, I said
and after you are well

you can do as you please.
She smiled, Yes
you do what you please first
then I can do what I please—

Oh, oh, oh! she cried
as the ambulance men lifted

her to the stretcher—
Is this what you call

making me comfortable?
By now her mind was clear—
Oh you think you're smart
you young people,

she said, but I'll tell you
you don't know anything.
Then we started.
On the way

we passed a long row
of elms. She looked at them
awhile out of
the ambulance window and said,

What are all those
fuzzy-looking things out there?
Trees? Well, I'm tired
of them and rolled her head away.

William Carlos Williams

REQUIEM
for Shanshan

The wave of that year
flooded the sands on the mirror
to be lost is a kind of leaving
and the meaning of leaving
the instant when all languages
are like shadows cast from the west

life's only a promise
don't grieve for it
before the garden was destroyed
we had too much time
debating the implications of a bird flying
as we knocked down midnight's door

alone like a match polished into light
when childhood's tunnel
led to a vein of dubious ore
to be lost is a kind of leaving
and poetry rectifying life
rectifies poetry's echo

Ryszard Krynicki
Translated from the Polish by Claire Cavanagh

FOR MY BROTHER: REPORTED
MISSING IN ACTION, 1943

Sweet brother, if I do not sleep
My eyes are flowers for your tomb;
And if I cannot eat my bread,
My fasts shall live like willows where you died.
If in the heat I find no water for my thirst,
My thirst shall turn to springs for you, poor
    traveller.

Where, in what desolate and smokey country,
Lies your poor body, lost and dead?
And in what landscape of disaster
Has your unhappy spirit lost its road?

Come, in my labor find a resting place
And in my sorrows lay your head,
Or rather take my life and blood
And buy yourself a better bed—
Or take my breath and take my death
And buy yourself a better rest.

When all the men of war are shot
And flags have fallen into dust,
Your cross and mine shall tell men still
Christ died on each, for both of us.

For in the wreckage of your April Christ lies slain,
And Christ weeps in the ruins of my spring:

The money of Whose tears shall fall
Into your weak and friendless hand,
And buy you back to your own land:
The silence of Whose tears shall fall
Like bells upon your alien tomb.
Hear them and come: they call you home.

Thomas Merton

CATULLUS 101

Sped through many countries and as many seas
I've come, dear brother, to attend your mourning
    rites
And bring the final tribute that a death requires,
Only to find myself addressing silent ashes.
Since fate has taken even you away from me—
Oh no, my brother, so unjustly stolen from me!—
Nevertheless, in keeping with our forebears'
    customs,
I tender grief's last offering to your memory
Drenched with fraternal tears of one who wept
    for you.
And now, for all time, Brother, this salute, and
    this farewell.

Catullus
Translated by Alfred Corn

from **IN MEMORIAM A.H.H.**
OBIT MDCCCXXXIII: 27

XI

Calm is the morn without a sound,
     Calm as to suit a calmer grief,
     And only through the faded leaf
The chestnut pattering to the ground:

Calm and deep peace on this high world,
     And on these dews that drench the furze,
     And all the silvery gossamers
That twinkle into green and gold:

Calm and still light on yon great plain
     That sweeps with all its autumn bowers,
     And crowded farms and lessening towers,
To mingle with the bounding main:

Calm and deep peace in this wide air,
     These leaves that redden to the fall;
     And in my heart, if calm at all,
If any calm, a calm despair:

Calm on the seas, and silver sleep,
     And waves that sway themselves in rest,
     And dead calm in that noble breast
Which heaves but with the heaving deep.

XXVII

I envy not in any moods
    The captive void of noble rage,
    The linnet born within the cage,
That never knew the summer woods:

I envy not the beast that takes
    His license in the field of time,
    Unfetter'd by the sense of crime,
To whom a conscience never wakes;

Nor, what may count itself as blest,
    The heart that never plighted troth
    But stagnates in the weeds of sloth;
Nor any want-begotten rest.

I hold it true, whate'er befall;
    I feel it, when I sorrow most;
    'Tis better to have loved and lost
Than never to have loved at all.

Alfred Lord Tennyson

A REFUSAL TO MOURN THE DEATH, BY FIRE, OF A CHILD IN LONDON

Never until the mankind making
Bird beast and flower
Fathering and all humbling darkness
Tells with silence the last light breaking
And the still hour
Is come of the sea tumbling in harness

And I must enter again the round
Zion of the water bead
And the synagogue of the ear of corn
Shall I let pray the shadow of a sound
Or sow my salt seed
In the least valley of sackcloth to mourn

The majesty and burning of the child's death.
I shall not murder
The mankind of her going with a grave truth
Nor blaspheme down the stations of the breath
With any further
Elegy of innocence and youth.

Deep with the first dead lies London's daughter,
Robed in the long friends,
The grains beyond age, the dark veins of her
    mother,

Secret by the unmourning water
Of the riding Thames.
After the first death, there is no other.

Dylan Thomas

REDEMPTION SONG

Finally fall.
At last the mist,
heat's haze, we woke
these past weeks with

has lifted. We find
ourselves chill, a briskness
we hug ourselves in.
Frost greying the ground.

Grief might be easy
if there wasn't still
such beauty—would be far
simpler if the silver

maple didn't thrust
its leaves into flame,
trusting that spring
will find it again.

All this might be easier if
there wasn't a song
still lifting us above it,
if wind didn't trouble

my mind like water.
I half expect to see you
fill the autumn air
like breath—

At night I sleep
on clenched fists.
Days I'm like the child
who on the playground

falls, crying
not so much from pain
as surprise.
I'm tired of tide

taking you away,
then back again—
what's worse, the forgetting
or the thing

you can't forget.
Neither yet—

last summer's
choir of crickets

grown quiet.

19 October

Kevin Young

LAST REQUESTS

are clear in books: "Dorset, embrace him …
And make me happy in your unity";
and in old movies: "Take care of my hyacinths."
In opera, last pleas fill the diva's arias.

I've waited for last hopes, my amulets
against silence. My father, dying, spoke
in an urgent Polish he'd not used in years,
but his words, staccato trumpet notes,

were not injunctions. When my mother's life
crested like a wave before it breaks,
I asked her wishes. She said, "Ice cream, quick!"
and hurled a glance that said she was not in pain

but dying, and must hurry on with it.
Lips trembled open: "Don't kiss me again.
No, you catch everything. But thanks for coming."
Then quiet. In a trance, a captive audience,

she could not stop my vows, but not a syllable
I uttered had been left unsaid in tiffs,
snarls at ogres in the stories told
on rainy days until the china mugs

rattled on glass shelves, in alphabet games,
nouns binding us like ropes we strung with beads
and lifted up, verbs spinning like bedsheets
we dried, then pulled taut. Words were for wishing

on first daffodils, secrets kept from others.
Now I'll take any edict, fiat, murmur,
gossip, or prayer. Hers, not another's.
When the phone rang at dawn I thought, wrong
    number,

and blurred the verdict. Even expecting it,
I was not prepared, nor will I be
in her rooms, tapping a crystal bowl,
waiting for words to burn through it like sun.

Grace Schulman

DIRGE

(from *Cymbeline*)

Fear no more the heat o' the sun,
Nor the furious winter's rages;
Thou thy worldly task hast done,
Home art gone, and ta'en thy wages:
Golden lads and girls all must,
As chimney-sweepers, come to dust.

Fear no more the frown o' the great;
Thou art past the tyrant's stroke;
Care no more to clothe and eat;
To thee the reed is as the oak:
The scepter, learning, physic, must
All follow this, and come to dust.

Fear no more the lightning flash,
Nor the all-dreaded thunder stone;
Fear not slander, censure rash;
Thou hast finished joy and moan:
All lovers young, all lovers must
Consign to thee, and come to dust.

No exorciser harm thee!
Nor no witchcraft charm thee!
Ghost unlaid forbear thee!

Nothing ill come near thee!
Quiet consummation have;
And renownèd be thy grave!

William Shakespeare

LYKE-WAKE DIRGE

This ae night, this ae night
Every night and alle,
Fire and flame and candle light
And Christ receive your soul.

When you're past and far away
Every night and alle,
To Whinny Moor you come at last
And Christ receive your soul.

If ever you gave socks or shoes
Every night and alle,
Sit you down and put them on
And Christ receive your soul.

If you gave no one socks or shoes
Every night and alle,
The wind will prick you to the bone
And Christ receive your soul.

When you pass the Bridge of Dread
Every night and alle,
To Purgatory you will come
And Christ receive your soul.

If you never gave food or drink
Every night and alle,

The fire will burn you to the bone
And Christ receive your soul.

Traditional English song,
modern version by GS

SHALL WE GATHER AT THE RIVER

Shall we gather at the river,
Where bright angel feet have trod,
With its crystal tide forever
Flowing by the throne of God.

Yes, we'll gather at the river,
The beautiful, the beautiful river;
Gather with the saints at the river
That flows by the throne of God

On the margin of the river,
Washing up its silver spray,
We will talk and worship ever,
All the happy golden day.

Ere we reach the shining river,
Lay we every burden down;
Grace our spirits will deliver,
And provide a robe and crown.

At the smiling of the river,
Mirror of the Savior's face,
Saints, whom death will never sever,
Lift their songs of saving grace.

Soon we'll reach the silver river,
Soon our pilgrimage will cease;
Soon our happy hearts will quiver
With the melody of peace.

Robert Lowry

WOMEN'S DANCE SONG

The owl cries out to me,
   the hawk cries out to me
as death approaches.

The killdeer, the mountain bird,
   cry out to me
as death approaches.

The red racer, the gartersnake
   cry out to me
as death approaches.

A large frog, a little frog,
   cry out to me
as death approaches.

An eagle, a condor,
   cry out to me
as death approaches.

Native American song-poem
of the Temecula people
adapted by Brian Swann

PSALM 23

The Lord is my shepherd; I shall not want.

He maketh me to lie down in green pastures; He leadeth me beside the still waters.

He restoreth my soul; He leadeth me in the paths of righteousness for His name's sake.

Yea, though I walk through the valley of the shadow of death, I will fear no evil; for Thou art with me; Thy rod and Thy staff, they comfort me.

Thou preparest a table before me in the presence of mine enemies; Thou anointest my head with oil; my cup runneth over.

Surely goodness and mercy shall follow me all the days of my life; and I will dwell in the house of the Lord for ever.

As the hart panteth after the water brooks, so
panteth my soul after thee, O God.

My soul thirsteth for God, for the living God:
when shall I come and appear before God?

My tears have been my meat day and night,
while they continually say unto me, Where is thy
God?

When I remember these things, I pour out my
soul in me: for I had gone with the multitude,
I went with them to the house of God, with the
voice of joy and praise, with a multitude that kept
holyday.

Why art thou cast down, O my soul? and why
art thou disquieted in me? hope thou in God:
for I shall yet praise him for the help of his
countenance.

O my God, my soul is cast down within me:
therefore will I remember thee from the land
of Jordan, and of the Hermonites, from the hill
Mizar.

Deep calleth unto deep at the noise of thy waterspouts: all thy waves and thy billows are gone over me.

Yet the Lord will command his lovingkindness in the day time, and in the night his song shall be with me, and my prayer unto the God of my life.

I will say unto God my rock, Why hast thou forgotten me? why go I mourning because of the oppression of the enemy?

As with a sword in my bones, mine enemies reproach me; while they say daily unto me, Where is thy God?

Why art thou cast down, O my soul? and why art thou disquieted within me? hope thou in God: for I shall yet praise him, who is the health of my countenance, and my God.

King James Version

KADDISH

Exalted and sanctified
be his great name in the world
created according to his plan;
may His majesty be revealed
during our days
and the life of all Israel,
speedily. Soon. Say, Amen.
Blessed is his name.
Blessed, praised, honored,
exalted, glorified, sanctified,
extolled, adored and lauded,
be the name of the Holy One,
blessed be He
beyond all earthly words
and songs of blessing,
hymns, praise and comfort.
Say amen.
May the one who creates harmony
bring peace, grace, lovingkindness
and compassion;
sustenance and salvation,
to us and to all humankind.
Say, Amen.

*Ancient Jewish prayer
recited in memory of the dead,
here adapted from the Aramaic.*

The Shape of Death

EVENING

The light passes
from ridge to ridge,
from flower to flower—
the hepaticas, wide-spread
under the light
grow faint—
the petals reach inward,
the blue tips bend
toward the bluer heart
and the flowers are lost.

The cornel-buds are still white,
but shadows dart
from the cornel-roots—
black creeps from root to root,
each leaf
cuts another leaf on the grass,
shadow seeks shadow,
then both leaf
and leaf-shadow are lost.

H. D. (Hilda Doolittle)

WHAT ARE YEARS

What is our innocence,
what is our guilt? All are
      naked, none is safe. And whence
is courage: the unanswered question,
the resolute doubt,—
dumbly calling, deafly listening—that
in misfortune, even death,
      encourage others
      and in its defeat, stirs

      the soul to be strong? He
sees deep and is glad, who
      accedes to mortality
and in his imprisonment rises
upon himself as
the sea in a chasm, struggling to be
free and unable to be,
      in its surrendering
      finds its continuing.

      So he who strongly feels,
behaves. The very bird,
      grown taller as he sings, steels
his form straight up. Though he is captive,
his mighty singing

says, satisfaction is a lowly
thing, how pure a thing is joy.
     This is mortality,
     this is eternity.

Marianne Moore

DEATH BE NOT PROUD

Death, be not proud, though some have called
    thee
Mighty and dreadful, for thou art not so;
For those whom thou think'st thou dost overthrow
Die not, poor Death, nor yet canst thou kill me.
From rest and sleep, which but thy pictures be,
Much pleasure; then from thee much more must
    flow,
And soonest our best men with thee do go,
Rest of their bones, and soul's delivery.
Thou art slave to fate, chance, kings, and
    desperate men,
And dost with poison, war, and sickness dwell,
And poppy or charms can make us sleep as well
And better than thy stroke; why swell'st thou then?
One short sleep past, we wake eternally
And death shall be no more; Death, thou shalt die.

John Donne

AFTER GREAT PAIN

After great pain, a formal feeling comes—
The Nerves sit ceremonious, like Tombs—
The stiff Heart questions 'was it He, that bore,'
And 'Yesterday, or Centuries before'?

The Feet, mechanical, go round—
A Wooden way
Of Ground, or Air, or Ought—
Regardless grown,
A Quartz contentment, like a stone—

This is the Hour of Lead—
Remembered, if outlived,
As Freezing persons, recollect the Snow—
First— Chill— then Stupor— then the letting go—

Emily Dickinson

AND DEATH SHALL HAVE NO DOMINION

And death shall have no dominion.
Dead man naked they shall be one
With the man in the wind and the west moon;
When their bones are picked clean and the clean
    bones gone,
They shall have stars at elbow and foot;
Though they go mad they shall be sane,
Though they sink through the sea they shall rise
    again;
Though lovers be lost love shall not;
And death shall have no dominion.

And death shall have no dominion.
Under the windings of the sea
They lying long shall not die windily;
Twisting on racks when sinews give way,
Strapped to a wheel, yet they shall not break;
Faith in their hands shall snap in two,
And the unicorn evils run them through;
Split all ends up they shan't crack;
And death shall have no dominion.

And death shall have no dominion.
No more may gulls cry at their ears
Or waves break loud on the seashores;
Where blew a flower may a flower no more
Lift its head to the blows of the rain;

Though they be mad and dead as nails,
Heads of the characters hammer through daisies;
Break in the sun till the sun breaks down,
And death shall have no dominion.

Dylan Thomas

BOOKS, PAINTINGS

Books, paintings, an amber necklace,
an apartment, if we live that long,
pupil of the sky's eye and a dewdrop,
tiger shell, passport, memory,
human homeland without armies or borders,
wedding rings, photos, manuscripts,
five liters of blood (together: ten), hunger,
dusks and the gift of morning,

we can lose everything,
everything can be taken from us

except the independent,
nameless words,
even if they only flow through us
except sacred word, which even
when written in dead languages of ice

will see resurrection

Ryszard Krynicki
Translated from the Polish
by Claire Cavanagh

IN THE HOME OF THE DEAD MAN

In the home of the dead man
the lights stay on till midnight
like toppled sand dunes
beneath a red sky
a flock of blackbirds.
A felt hat left behind
by the last visitor
coffee rank
as the darkened armpits
of men wearing white shirts.
With the greatest ease this afternoon
we launched a boat into black waters
and cried: "Swim!"

In the home of the dead man
a bed is missing.
So is a wooden stake from the yard—
details nobody has noticed.
Gone too are the stars
the shepherd once with his crook
drove across the sky
to keep them away
from gardens and houses.

Luljeta Lleshanaku
Translated from the Albanian
by Henry Israeli

QUESTION

Body my house
my horse my hound
what will I do
when you are fallen

Where will I sleep
How will I ride
What will I hunt

Where can I go
without my mount
all eager and quick
How will I know
in thicket ahead
is danger or treasure
when Body my good
bright dog is dead

How will it be
to lie in the sky
without roof or door
and wind for an eye

With cloud for shift
how will I hide?

May Swenson

Talking to Grief

CHAMOMILE BREATH

We never talk about death, mother
like married people who never speak of sex
doctors who never mention blood
the postman who no longer realizes he is holding
    his breath.

But fear of it graces everything you touch
the way a cotton field quivers
as a man strides through it.

In the morning
your chamomile breath
rises over the wrinkled pillow
adorned with white ubiquitous strands of hair
and black metal clips.

Don't wait for death to come noisily, mother,
dressed in wild, colored cloth
bells on its elbows and knees
like the Man of Carnivals
or a morris dancer at the end of May.

You will see instead a child with spindly legs /
    and a thick crop of hair
a child who never had the chance to grow up.

Haven't you heard the saying:
death is so close to birth
they are like nostrils on a face
letting out a sneeze.

Luljeta Lleshanaku
translated from the Albanian
by Henry Israeli

TALKING TO GRIEF

Ah, Grief, I should not treat you
like a homeless dog
who comes to the back door
for a crust, for a meatless bone.
I should trust you.

I should coax you
into the house and give you
your own corner,
a worn mat to lie on,
your own water dish.

You think I don't know you've been living
under my porch.
You long for your real place to be readied
before winter comes. You need
your name,
your collar and tag. You need
the right to warn off intruders,
to consider
my house your own
and me your person
and yourself
my own dog.

Denise Levertov

RIDER'S SONG

Córdoba.
Far away and alone.
Black pony, big moon,
and olives in my saddle-bag.
Although I know the roads
I'll never reach Córdoba.
Through the plain, through the wind,
black pony, red moon.
Death is looking at me
from the towers of Córdoba.
Ay! How long the road!
Ay! My valiant pony!
Ay! That death should wait me
before I reach Córdoba.
Córdoba.
Far away and alone.

Federico García Lorca
Translated by Stephen Spender and J. L. Gili

NO WORST, THERE IS NONE

No worst, there is none. Pitched past pitch of grief,
More pangs will, schooled at forepangs, wilder
    wring.
Comforter, where, where is your comforting?
Mary, mother of us, where is your relief?
My cries heave, herds-long; huddle in a main, a
    chief
Woe, wórld-sorrow; on an áge-old anvil wince and
    sing—
Then lull, then leave off. Fury had shrieked 'No
    ling-
ering! Let me be fell: force I must be brief.'"

    O the mind, mind has mountains; cliffs of fall
Frightful, sheer, no-man-fathomed. Hold them
    cheap
May who ne'er hung there. Nor does long our
    small
Durance deal with that steep or deep. Here! creep,
Wretch, under a comfort serves in a whirlwind: all
Life death does end and each day dies with sleep.

Gerard Manley Hopkins

When I have fears that I may cease to be
    Before my pen has gleaned my teeming
      brain,
Before high-pilèd books, in charactery,
    Hold like rich garners the full ripened grain;
When I behold, upon the night's starred face,
    Huge cloudy symbols of a high romance,
And think that I may never live to trace
    Their shadows with the magic hand of
      chance;
And when I feel, fair creature of an hour,
    That I shall never look upon thee more,
Never have relish in the faery power
    Of unreflecting love—then on the shore
Of the wide world I stand alone, and think
Till love and fame to nothingness do sink.

John Keats

NOT TO DIE NOW

Not to die now but sometime after this,
In a larger room, elsewhere, in fresher air,
Some place favored in memory, perhaps a hill

Among the bleaching bones of sheep, hawk-
    killed,
With the cuckoo's muted horn in ear,
A pleasure boat below reaching for open sea-

A moment when the wind rises or falls.
But not as I now am, wearied out upon
The fool's errand I have sent myself.

Allen Grossman

ONLY DEATH

There are lone cemeteries,
tombs filled with soundless bones,
the heart passing through a tunnel
dark, dark, dark;
like a shipwreck we die inward,
like smothering in our hearts,
like slowly falling from our skin down to our soul.

There are corpses,
there are feet of sticky, cold gravestone,
there is death in the bones,
like a pure sound,
like a bark without a dog,
coming from certain bells, from certain tombs,
growing in the dampness like teardrops or
        raindrops.

I see alone, at times,
coffins with sails
weighing anchor with pale corpses, with dead-
        tressed women,
with bakers white as angels,
with pensive girls married to notaries,
coffins going up the vertical river of the dead,
the dark purple river,

upward, with the sails swollen by the sound
     of death,
swollen by the silent sound of death.

To resonance comes death
like a shoe without a foot, like a suit without a man,
she comes to knock with a stoneless and
     fingerless ring,
she comes to shout without mouth, without
     tongue, without throat.
Yet her steps sound
and her dress sounds, silent as a tree.

I know little, I am not well acquainted, I can
     scarcely see,
but I think that her song has the color of moist
     violets,
of violets accustomed to the earth,
because the face of death is green,
and the gaze of death is green,
with the sharp dampness of a violet leaf
and its dark color of exasperated winter.

But death also goes through the world dressed as
     a broom,

she licks the ground looking for corpses,
death is in the broom,
it is death's tongue looking for dead bodies,
it is death's needle looking for thread.

Death is in the cots:
in the slow mattresses, in the black blankets
she lives stretched out, and she suddenly blows:
she blows a dark sound that puffs out sheets,
and there are beds sailing to a port
where she is waiting, dressed as an admiral.

Pablo Neruda

NOTING GOLD CAN STAY

Nature's first green is gold,
Her hardest hue to hold.
Her early leaf's a flower;
But only so an hour.
Then leaf subsides to leaf,
So Eden sank to grief,
So dawn goes down to day
Nothing gold can stay.

Robert Frost

I LIVE YET DO NOT LIVE IN ME

I live yet do not live in me,
am waiting as my life goes by,
and die because I do not die.

No longer do I live in me,
and without God I cannot live;
to him or me I cannot give
my self, so what can living be?
A thousand deaths my agony
waiting as my life goes by,
dying because I do not die.

This life I live alone I view
as robbery of life, and so
it is a constant death—with no
way out until I live with you.
God, hear me, what I say is true:
I do not want this life of mine,
and die because I do not die.

Being so removed from you I say
what kind of life can I have here
but death so ugly and severe
and worse than any form of pain?
I pity me—and yet my fate
is that I must keep up this lie,
and die because I do not die.

The fish taken out of the sea
is not without a consolation:
his dying is of brief duration
and ultimately brings relief.
Yet what convulsive death can be
as bad as my pathetic life?
The more I live the more I die.

When I begin to feel relief
on seeing you in the sacrament,
I sink in deeper discontent,
deprived of your sweet company.
Now everything compels my grief:
I want—yet can't—see you nearby,
and die because I do not die.

Although I find my pleasure, Sir,
in hope of someday seeing you,
I see that I can lose you too,
which makes my pain doubly severe,
and so I live in darkest fear,
and hope, wait as life goes by,
dying because I do not die.

Deliver me from death, my God,
and give me life; now you have wound
a rope about me; harshly bound

I ask you to release the cord.
See how I die to see you, Lord,
and I am shattered where I lie,
dying because I do not die.

My death will trigger tears in me,
and I shall mourn my life: a day
annihilated by the way
I fail and sin relentlessly.
O Father God, when will it be
that I can say without a lie:
I live because I do not die?

St. John of the Cross
Translated from the Spanish
by Willis Barnstone

A LAMENTATION

Grief, have I denied thee?
Grief, I have denied thee.

That robe or tunic, black gauze
over black and silver my sister wore
to dance *Sorrow*, hung so long
in my closet. I never tried it on.
      And my dance
was *Summer*—they rouged my cheeks
and twisted roses with wire stems into my hair.
I was compliant, Juno de sept ans,
betraying my autumn birthright pour faire
      plaisir.
Always denial. Grief in the morning, washed
      away
in coffee, crumbled to a dozen errands between
busy fingers.

      Or across cloistral shadow, insistent
intrusion of pink sunstripes from open
archways, falling recurrent.

Corrosion denied, the figures the acid designs
filled in. Grief dismissed,
the Eros along with grief.
Phantasmagoria swept across the sky
by shaky winds endlessly,

the spaces of blue timidly steady—
blue curtains at trailer windows framing
the cinder walks.
There are hidden corners of sky
choked with the swept shreds, with pain and
      ashes.

                                 Grief,
have I denied thee? Denied thee.
The emblems torn from the walls,
and the black plumes.

Denise Levertov

HOW DO I LOVE THEE
Sonnet 46

How do I love thee? Let me count the ways.
I love thee to the depth and breadth and height
My soul can reach, when feeling out of sight
For the ends of being and ideal grace.
I love thee to the level of every day's
Most quiet need, by sun and candle-light.
I love thee freely, as men strive for right;
I love thee purely, as they turn from praise.
I love thee with the passion put to use
In my old griefs, and with my childhood's faith.
I love thee with a love I seemed to lose
With my lost saints. I love thee with the breath,
Smiles, tears, of all my life; and, if God choose,
I shall but love thee better after death.

Elizabeth Barrett Browning

THE HEAVY BEAR WHO GOES WITH ME

"the withness of the body"

The heavy bear who goes with me,
A manifold honey to smear his face,
Clumsy and lumbering here and there,
The central ton of every place,
The hungry beating brutish one
In love with candy, anger, and sleep,
Crazy factotum, dishevelling all,
Climbs the building, kicks the football,
Boxes his brother in the hate-ridden city.

Breathing at my side, that heavy animal,
That heavy bear who sleeps with me,
Howls in his sleep for a world of sugar,
A sweetness intimate as the water's clasp,
Howls in his sleep because the tight-rope
Trembles and shows the darkness beneath.
—The strutting show-off is terrified,
Dressed in his dress-suit, bulging his pants,
Trembles to think that his quivering meat
Must finally wince to nothing at all.

That inescapable animal walks with me,
Has followed me since the black womb held,
Moves where I move, distorting my gesture,
A caricature, a swollen shadow,

A stupid clown of the spirit's motive,
Perplexes and affronts with his own darkness,
The secret life of belly and bone,
Opaque, too near, my private, yet unknown,
Stretches to embrace the very dear
With whom I would walk without him near,
Touches her grossly, although a word
Would bare my heart and make me clear,
Stumbles, flounders, and strives to be fed
Dragging me with him in his mouthing care,
Amid the hundred million of his kind,
The scrimmage of appetite everywhere.

Delmore Schwartz

End of Days

THIS LIVING HAND, NOW WARM AND CAPABLE

This living hand, now warm and capable
Of earnest grasping, would, if it were cold
And in the icy silence of the tomb,
So haunt thy days and chill thy dreaming nights
That thou would wish thine own heart dry of
     blood
So in my veins red life might stream again,
And thou be conscience-calmed–see here it is–
I hold it towards you.

John Keats

EVEN SUCH IS TIME

Even such is time, which takes in trust
Our youth, our joys, and all we have,
And pays us but with age and dust,
Who in the dark and silent grave
When we have wandered all our ways
Shuts up the story of our days,
And from which earth, and grave, and dust
The Lord will raise me up, I trust.

Sir Walter Raleigh

REQUIEM

Under the wide and starry sky
Dig the grave and let me lie:
Glad did I live and gladly die,
And I laid me down with a will.

This be the verse you 'grave for me:
Here he lies where he longed to be;
Home is the sailor, home from the sea,
And the hunter home from the hill.

Robert Louis Stevenson

EPITAPH

Stop, Christian passer-by!—Stop, child of God,
And read with gentle breast. Beneath this sod
A poet lies, or that which once seemed he.
O, lift one thought in prayer for S. T. C.;
That he who many a year with toil of breath
Found death in life, may here find life in death!
Mercy for praise—to be forgiven for fame
He asked, and hoped, through Christ. Do thou
    the same!

Samuel Taylor Coleridge

LAST REQUEST

Bury me in a cocoa pod, it's time.
Bury me in a Mercedes Benz, a
silver one, I've met my end.
Bury me in a lobster shell, a

carapace of red, now I'm dead.
Bury me in a jet marked KLM,
a typewriter labeled Remington,
a stove-in boat, symbol of my clan.

Bury me in a pot of India ink,
only place that I can think.
Bury me in a skull in Voronezh
that dreams of dragonflies

and the spider's web, heaped
hills of human heads, since I'm dead.
Bury me in a can of flammable film
with Keaton (Buster) and Beckett (Sam).

Bury me in Little Boy and in Fat Man,
plunging toward the edge of time.
A cuckoo clock, a block
of bluest ice. Quincunx, Devil's Trill,

or 22 June, Town Hall, '45.
Lay me beside her in the Song of Songs,

our limbs forever intertwined,
now that I'm not alive.

Or plant me with the poets in an opium pipe,
its glowing ring of light.

Stick me in the ground
without a thought without a sound.

Michael Palmer

from **DOCTOR FAUSTUS**

FAUSTUS: Ah, Faustus,
Now hast thou but one bare hour to live,
And then thou must be damned perpetually!
Stand still, you ever-moving spheres of heaven,
That time may cease, and midnight never come;
Fair nature's eye, rise, rise again, and make
Perpetual day; or let this hour be but
A year, a month, a week, a natural day,
That Faustus may repent and save his soul!
O lente, lente currite, noctis equi!
The stars move still, time runs, the clock will
    strike,
The devil will come, and Faustus must be
    damned.
O, I'll leap up to my God!— Who pulls me
    down?—
See, see, where Christ's blood streams in the
    firmament!
One drop would save my soul, half a drop: ah, my
    Christ!—
Rend not my heart for naming of my Christ!
Yet will I call on him: O, spare me, Lucifer!—
Where is it now? 'Tis gone:
And see, where God stretcheth out his arm,
And bends his ireful brows!
Mountains and hills, come, come, and fall on me,
And hide me from the heavy wrath of God!

No, no!
Then will I headlong run into the earth.
Earth, gape! O no, it will not harbour me!
You stars that reigned at my nativity,
Whose influence hath allotted death and hell,
Now draw up Faustus, like a foggy mist.
Into the entrails of yon labouring clouds,
That, when they vomit forth into the air,
My limbs may issue from their smoky mouths,
So that my soul may but ascend to heaven!

[The clock strikes.]

Ah, half the hour is past! 'twill all be past anon
O God,
If thou wilt not have mercy on my soul,
Yet for Christ's sake, whose blood hath ransomed
    me,
Impose some end to my incessant pain;
Let Faustus live in hell a thousand years,
A hundred thousand, and at last be saved!
O, no end is limited to damned souls!
Why wert thou not a creature wanting soul?
Or why is this immortal that thou hast?
Ah, Pythagoras' metempsychosis, were that true,
This soul should fly from me, and I be changed
Unto some brutish beast! all beasts are happy,
For, when they die,
Their souls are soon dissolved in elements;

But mine must live still to be plagued in hell.
Cursed be the parents that engendered me!
No, Faustus, curse thyself, curse Lucifer
That hath deprived thee of the joys of heaven.
                    [The clock strikes.]
O, it strikes, it strikes! Now, body, turn to air,
Or Lucifer will bear thee quick to hell!
                    [Thunder and lightning.]
O soul, be changed into little water-drops,
And fall into the ocean, ne'er be found!
                    [Enter DEVILS.]
My God, my god, look not so fierce on me!
Adders and serpents, let me breathe a while!
Ugly hell, gape not! come not, Lucifer!
I'll burn my books!— Ah, Mephistopheles!
                    [Exeunt DEVILS with FAUSTUS]

For the Masters

SEPTEMBER 1961

This is the year the old ones,
the old great ones
leave us alone on the road.

The road leads to the sea.
We have the words in our pockets,
obscure directions. The old ones

have taken away the light of their presence,
we see it moving away over a hill
off to one side.

They are not dying,
they are withdrawn
into a painful privacy

learning to live without words.
E. P. "It looks like dying"—Williams: "I can't
describe to you what has been

happening to me"—
H. D. "unable to speak."
The darkness

twists itself in the wind, the stars
are small, the horizon
ringed with confused urban light-haze.

They have told us
the road leads to the sea,
and given

the language into our hands.
We hear
our footsteps each time a truck

has dazzled past us and gone
leaving us new silence.
One can't reach

the sea on this endless
road to the sea unless
one turns aside at the end, it seems,

follows
the owl that silently glides above it
aslant, back and forth,

and away into deep woods.

But for us the road
unfurls itself, we count the
words in our pockets, we wonder

how it will be without them, we don't
stop walking, we know
there is far to go, sometimes

we think the night wind carries
a smell of the sea.

Denise Levertov

JOSEPH BRODSKY'S GRAVE

Where the greasy sea
licks the gates.

In the evangelical section
near Ezra Pound
and Olga Rudge.

Faithful guests vanish:
an aggressive gull,
timid lizards.

At the base,
beneath a guttered votive,
someone has placed
(in a plastic sleeve
to keep out the rain)
a computer print-out photo:

Brodsky, ill, gaunt,
in front of the four tetrarchs.

Whole in his
intent gaze.
On the grave, oblations:

an upturned tumbler with small coins,
an empty vodka bottle

with a faded label,
twists of paper
tucked in greenery
(poems maybe? letters?
petitions? curses?)

A plastic bucket
full of ballpoints

(enough for another
far longer life).

Black plastic glasses

(plastic again,
the mark of time).

Pebbles on the gravestone,
as on a macewa, a Jewish tomb,

a pinecone, a little leaf.

Ryszard Krynicki
Translated from the Polish by Claire Cavanagh

ELEGY FOR THELONIOUS

Damn the snow.
Its senseless beauty
pours a hard light
through the hemlock.
Thelonious is dead. Winter
drifts in the hourglass;
notes pour from the brain cup.
damn the alley cat
wailing a muted dirge
off Lenox Ave.
Thelonious is dead.
Tonight's a lazy rhapsody of shadows
swaying to blue vertigo
& metaphysical funk.
Black trees in the wind.
Crepuscule with Nellie
plays inside the bowed head.
"Dig the Man Ray of piano!"
O Satisfaction,
hot fingers blur on those white rib keys.
Coming on the Hudson.
Monk's Dream.
The ghost of bebop
from 52nd Street,
footprints in the snow.
Damn February.
Let's go to Minton's

& play "modern malice"
till daybreak. Lord,
there's Thelonious
wearing that old funky hat
pulled down over his eyes.

Yusef Komunyakaa

AT MELVILLE'S TOMB

Often beneath the wave, wide from this ledge
The dice of drowned men's bones he saw
    bequeath
An embassy. Their numbers as he watched,
Beat on the dusty shore and were obscured.

And wrecks passed without sound of bells,
The calyx of death's bounty giving back
A scattered chapter, livid hieroglyph,
The portent wound in corridors of shells.

Then in the circuit calm of one vast coil,
Its lashings charmed and malice reconciled,
Frosted eyes there were that lifted altars;
And silent answers crept across the stars.

Compass, quadrant and sextant contrive
No farther tides … High in the azure steeps
Monody shall not wake the mariner.
This fabulous shadow only the sea keeps.

Hart Crane

IN MEMORY OF W. B. YEATS

I

He disappeared in the dead of winter:
The brooks were frozen, the airports almost
    deserted,
And snow disfigured the public statues;
The mercury sank in the mouth of the dying day.
What instruments we have agree
The day of his death was a dark cold day.

Far from his illness
The wolves ran on through the evergreen forests,
The peasant river was untempted by the
    fashionable quays;
By mourning tongues
The death of the poet was kept from his poems.

But for him it was his last afternoon as himself,
An afternoon of nurses and rumours;
The provinces of his body revolted,
The squares of his mind were empty,
Silence invaded the suburbs,
The current of his feeling failed; he became his
    admirers.

Now he is scattered among a hundred cities
And wholly given over to unfamiliar affections,
To find his happiness in another kind of wood
And be punished under a foreign code of conscience.

The words of a dead man
Are modified in the guts of the living.

But in the importance and noise of to-morrow
When the brokers are roaring like beasts on the
    floor of the Bourse,
And the poor have the sufferings to which they are
    fairly accustomed,
And each in the cell of himself is almost
    convinced of his freedom,
A few thousand will think of this day
As one thinks of a day when one did something
    slightly unusual.

What instruments we have agree
The day of his death was a dark cold day.

II

You were silly like us; your gift survived it all:
The parish of rich women, physical decay,
Yourself. Mad Ireland hurt you into poetry.
Now Ireland has her madness and her weather still,
For poetry makes nothing happen: it survives
In the valley of its making where executives
Would never want to tamper, flows on south
From ranches of isolation and the busy griefs,

Raw towns that we believe and die in; it survives,
A way of happening, a mouth.

III

Earth, receive an honoured guest:
William Yeats is laid to rest.
Let the Irish vessel lie
Emptied of its poetry.

Time that is intolerant
Of the brave and the innocent,
And indifferent in a week
To a beautiful physique,

Worships language and forgives
Everyone by whom it lives;
Pardons cowardice, conceit,
Lays its honours at their feet.

Time that with this strange excuse
Pardoned Kipling and his views,
And will pardon Paul Claudel,
Pardons him for writing well.

In the nightmare of the dark
All the dogs of Europe bark,

And the living nations wait,
Each sequestered in its hate;

Intellectual disgrace
Stares from every human face,
And the seas of pity lie
Locked and frozen in each eye.

Follow, poet, follow right
To the bottom of the night,
With your unconstraining voice
Still persuade us to rejoice;

With the farming of a verse
Make a vineyard of the curse,
Sing of human unsuccess
In a rapture of distress;

In the deserts of the heart
Let the healing fountains start,
In the prison of his days
Teach the free man how to praise.

W. H. Auden

from **WHEN LILACS LAST IN THE DOORYARD BLOOM'D** *

1

When lilacs last in the dooryard bloom'd,
And the great star early droop'd in the western
    sky in the night,
I mourn'd, and yet shall mourn with ever-
    returning spring.

Ever-returning spring, trinity sure to me you
    bring,
Lilac blooming perennial and drooping star in
    the west,
And thought of him I love.

2

O powerful western fallen star!
O shades of night—O moody, tearful night!
O great star disappear'd—O the black murk that
    hides the star!
O cruel hands that hold me powerless—O
    helpless soul of me!
O harsh surrounding cloud that will not free my
    soul.

* *The poem is an elegy for Abraham Lincoln, although it does not refer to him by name.*

3

In the dooryard fronting an old farm-house near
    the white-washed palings,
Stands the lilac-bush tall-growing with heart-
    shaped leaves of rich green,
With many a pointed blossom rising delicate,
    with the perfume strong I love,
With every leaf a miracle—and from this bush in
    the dooryard,
With delicate-color'd blossoms and heart-shaped
    leaves of rich green,
A sprig with its flower I break.

4

In the swamp in secluded recesses,
A shy and hidden bird is warbling a song.

Solitary the thrush,
The hermit withdrawn to himself, avoiding the
    settlements,
Sings by himself a song.

Song of the bleeding throat,
Death's outlet song of life, (for well dear brother
    I know,
If thou wast not granted to sing thou would'st
    surely die.)

5

Over the breast of the spring, the land, amid cities,
Amid lanes and through old woods, where lately
    the violets peep'd from the ground, spotting
    the gray debris,
Amid the grass in the fields each side of the
    lanes, passing the endless grass,
Passing the yellow-spear'd wheat, every grain
    from its shroud in the dark-brown fields
    uprisen,
Passing the apple-tree blows of white and pink in
    the orchards,
Carrying a corpse to where it shall rest in the
    grave,
Night and day journeys a coffin.

6

Coffin that passes through lanes and streets,
Through day and night with the great cloud
    darkening the land,
With the pomp of the inloop'd flags with the
    cities draped in black,
With the show of the States themselves as of
    crape-veil'd women standing,
With processions long and winding and the
    flambeaus of the night,

With the countless torches lit, with the silent sea
     of faces and the unbared heads,
With the waiting depot, the arriving coffin, and
     the sombre faces,
With dirges through the night, with the thousand
     voices rising strong and solemn,
With all the mournful voices of the dirges pour'd
     around the coffin,
The dim-lit churches and the shuddering
     organs—where amid these you journey,
With the tolling tolling bells' perpetual clang,
Here, coffin that slowly passes,
I give you my sprig of lilac.

Walt Whitman

For the World

REQUIEM

for the victims of June Fourth *

Not the living but the dead
under the doomsday-purple sky
go in groups
suffering guides forward suffering
at the end of hatred is hatred
the spring has run dry, the conflagration
    stretches unbroken
the road back is even further away
Not gods but the children
amid the clashing of helmets
say their prayers
mothers breed light
darkness breeds mothers
the stone rolls, the clock runs backwards
the eclipse of the sun has already taken place
Not your bodies but your souls
share a common birthday every year
you are all the same age
love has founded for the dead

* *On June 4, 1989, many unarmed civilians were murdered during
a student-led protest in Tiananmen Square in Beijing, China.*

an everlasting alliance
you embrace each other closely
in the massive register of deaths

Bei Dao
Translated from the Chinese
by Eliot Weinberger

WHAT WERE THEY LIKE

1) Did the people of Viet Nam
   use lanterns of stone?
2) Did they hold ceremonies
   to reverence the opening of buds?
3) Were they inclined to quiet laughter?
4) Did they use bone and ivory,
   jade and silver, for ornament?
5) Had they an epic poem?
6) Did they distinguish between speech and
   singing?

1) Sir, their light hearts turned to stone.
   It is not remembered whether in gardens
   stone gardens illumined pleasant ways.
2) Perhaps they gathered once to delight in
      blossom,
   but after their children were killed
   there were no more buds.
3) Sir, laughter is bitter to the burned mouth.
4) A dream ago, perhaps. Ornament is for joy.
   All the bones were charred.
5) It is not remembered. Remember,
   most were peasants; their life
   was in rice and bamboo.
   When peaceful clouds were reflected in the
      paddies

and the water buffalo stepped surely along terraces,
maybe fathers told their sons old tales.
When bombs smashed those mirrors
there was time only to scream.

6) There is an echo yet
of their speech which was like a song.
It was reported their singing resembled
the flight of moths in moonlight.
Who can say? It is silent now.

Denise Levertov

ANTHEM FOR DOOMED YOUTH

What passing-bells for these who die as cattle?
    —Only the monstrous anger of the guns.
    Only the stuttering rifles' rapid rattle
Can patter out their hasty orisons.
No mockeries now for them; no prayers nor bells;
    Nor any voice of mourning save the choirs,—
The shrill, demented choirs of wailing shells;
    And bugles calling for them from sad shires.

What candles may be held to speed them all?
    Not in the hands of boys, but in their eyes
Shall shine the holy glimmers of goodbyes.
    The pallor of girls' brows shall be their pall;
Their flowers the tenderness of patient minds,
And each slow dusk a drawing-down of blinds.

Wilfred Owen

A LITANY IN TIME OF PLAGUE

Adieu, farewell earth's bliss,
This world uncertain is;
Fond are life's lustful joys,
Death proves them all but toys,
None from his darts can fly.
I am sick, I must die.
  Lord, have mercy on us!

Rich men, trust not in wealth,
Gold cannot buy you health;
Physic himself must fade,
All things to end are made.
The plague full swift goes by;
I am sick, I must die.
  Lord, have mercy on us!

Beauty is but a flower
Which wrinkles will devour;
Brightness falls from the air,
Queens have died young and fair,
Dust hath closed Helen's eye.
I am sick, I must die.
  Lord, have mercy on us!

Strength stoops unto the grave,
Worms feed on Hector brave,
Swords may not fight with fate.

Earth still holds ope her gate;
Come! come! the bells do cry.
I am sick, I must die.
Lord have mercy on us!

Thomas Nashe

CAMPO DEI FIORI

In Rome on the Campo dei Fiori
baskets of olives and lemons,
cobbles spattered with wine
and the wreckage of flowers.
Vendors cover the trestles
with rose-pink fish;
armfuls of dark grapes
heaped on peach-down.

On this same square
they burned Giordano Bruno.
Henchmen kindled the pyre
close-pressed by the mob.
Before the flames had died
the taverns were full again,
baskets of olives and lemons
again on the vendors' shoulders.

I thought of the Campo dei Fiori
in Warsaw by the sky-carousel
one clear spring evening
to the strains of a carnival tune.
The bright melody drowned
the salvos from the ghetto wall,
and couples were flying
high in the cloudless sky.

At times wind from the burning
would drift dark kites along
and riders on the carousel
caught petals in midair.
That same hot wind
blew open the skirts of the girls
and the crowds were laughing
on that beautiful Warsaw Sunday.

Someone will read as moral
that the people of Rome or Warsaw
haggle, laugh, make love
as they pass by the martyrs' pyres.
Someone else will read
of the passing of things human,
of the oblivion
born before the flames have died.

But that day I thought only
of the loneliness of the dying,
of how, when Giordano
climbed to his burning
he could not find
in any human tongue
words for mankind,
mankind who live on.

Already they were back at their wine
or peddled their white starfish,
baskets of olives and lemons
they had shouldered to the fair,
and he already distanced
as if centuries had passed
while they paused just a moment
for his flying in the fire.

Those dying here, the lonely
forgotten by the world,
our tongue becomes for them
the language of an ancient planet.
Until, when all is legend
and many years have passed,
on a new Campo dei Fiori
rage will kindle at a poet's word.

Warsaw, 1943

Czeslaw Milosz
Translated from the Polish
by David Brooks and Louis Iribarne

RECONCILIATION

Word over all, beautiful as the sky!
Beautiful that war, and all its deeds of carnage,
      must in time be utterly lost;
That the hands of the sisters Death and Night,
      incessantly softly wash again, and ever
      again, this soil'd world:
… For my enemy is dead—a man divine as myself
      is dead;
I look where he lies, white-faced and still, in the
      coffin—I draw near;
I bend down and touch lightly with my lips the
      white face in the coffin.

Walt Whitman

TO A DOG INJURED IN THE STREET

It is myself,
        not the poor beast lying there
                yelping with pain
that brings me to myself with a start—
        as at the explosion
                of a bomb, a bomb that has laid
all the world waste.
        I can do nothing
                but sing about it
and so I am assuaged
        from my pain.

A drowsy numbness drowns my sense
        as if of hemlock
                I had drunk. I think
of the poetry
        of René Char
                and all he must have seen
and suffered
        that has brought him
                to speak only of
sedgy rivers,
        of daffodils and tulips
                whose roots they water,
even to the free-flowing river
        that laves the rootlets
                of those sweet-scented flowers

that people the
    milky
        way.

I remember Norma
    our English setter of my childhood
        her silky ears
and expressive eyes.
    She had a litter
        of pups one night
in our pantry and I kicked
    one of them
        thinking, in my alarm,
that they
    were biting her breasts
        to destroy her.

I remember also
    a dead rabbit
        lying harmlessly
on the outspread palm
    of a hunter's hand.
        As I stood by
watching
    he took a hunting knife
        and with a laugh

thrust it
        up into the animal's private parts.
           I almost fainted.

Why should I think of that now?
        The cries of a dying dog
            are to be blotted out
as best I can.
        René Char
            you are a poet who believes
in the power of beauty
        to right all wrongs.
            I believe it also.
With invention and courage
        we shall surpass
            the pitiful dumb beasts,
let all men believe it,
        as you have taught me also
            to believe it.

William Carlos Williams

THE DARKLING THRUSH

I leant upon a coppice gate
    When Frost was spectre-grey,
And Winter's dregs made desolate
    The weakening eye of day.
The tangled bine-stems scored the sky
    Like strings of broken lyres,
And all mankind that haunted nigh
    Had sought their household fires.

The land's sharp features seemed to be
    The Century's corpse outleant,
His crypt the cloudy canopy,
    The wind his death-lament.
The ancient pulse of germ and birth
    Was shrunken hard and dry,
And every spirit upon earth
    Seemed fervourless as I.

At once a voice arose among
    The bleak twigs overhead
In a full-hearted evensong
    Of joy illimited;
An aged thrush, frail, gaunt, and small,
    In blast-beruffled plume,
Had chosen thus to fling his soul
    Upon the growing gloom.

So little cause for carolings
      Of such ecstatic sound
Was written on terrestrial things
      Afar or nigh around,
That I could think there trembled through
      His happy good-night air
Some blessed Hope, whereof he knew
      And I was unaware.

Thomas Hardy

Acknowledgments & permissions

"Woman's Dance Song," a Temecula song-poem, version by Brian Swann. From *Song of the Sky*. Copyright © 1993 University of Massachusetts Press.

"In Memory of W. B. Yeats," copyright 1940 and © renewed 1968 by W. H. Auden; from *Collected Poems* by W. H. Auden. Used by permission of Random House, an imprint and division of Penguin Random House LLC. All rights reserved.

"Requiem" from *Old Snow* by Bei Dao, copyright © 1991 by Bei Dao. Translation copyright © 1991 by Bonnie S. McDougall and Chen Maiping. Published in the UK by Carcanet Press Limited.

"Sestina" from *Poems* by Elizabeth Bishop. Copyright © 2011 by the Alice H. Methfessel Trust. Reprinted by permission of Farrar, Straus and Giroux. Used by permission of Penguin Books, Ltd.

"The Rites for Cousin Vit" by Gwendolyn Brooks. Reprinted by consent of Brooks Permissions.

"Evening" from *Collected Poems* by H. D., copyright © 1982 by the Estate of Hilda Doolittle. Published in the UK by Carcanet Press Limited.

"Elegy for Thelonious" from *Pleasure Dome: New and Collected Poems* © 2001 by Yusef Komunyakaa. Published by Wesleyan University Press and reprinted by permission.

"Mourning Chao" from *The Selected Poems of Li Po* by Li Po, translated by David Hinton, copyright © 1996 by David Hinton. Published in the UK by Carcanet Press Limited.